Theodore Roosevelt

A Biography of an American President

Table of Contents

Introduction

"Nothing in this world is worth having or worth doing unless it means effort, pain, difficulty." —Theodore Roosevelt

* * *

As the number of presidents increased from the United States' early days, after independence into the 20th century, it became difficult for any one president to stand out among the rest. From the perspective of the presidency, many great men have come and gone, all unique in their origins and personas and who had many achievements during their careers. So, what makes a president truly "great"? It is a great testimony to the permeable nature of American Democracy that one can look at those who have come to power and see how their individuality contributed to their significance.

Abraham Lincoln, for example, rose from simple origins, had little background in conventional education, and limited access to the bare minimum necessities to get by in life. His company was not composed of the American elite. He was, by all accounts, a humble man who rose to greatness by virtue of sheer industrious skill and his ability to capture the attention of people from all walks of American life.

Theodore Roosevelt, who would rise to become the 26th President of the United States, had a lot in common with Lincoln. Both were men of power and vitality; both had a similar command over the common people. Roosevelt's childhood, however, came with a number of advantages that Lincoln never had access to. Roosevelt came from New York City and was part of a family that had commanded respect for generations. His father was well known for his wealth and altruism.

American politics, it's important to note, is nothing if not a subtle balance of power and influence. Anything can become an advantage or a disadvantage, depending on how you choose to play it. Lincoln chose to transform his adversities into skills that catapulted him into the limelight, while Roosevelt refused to let his privileged upbringing lull him into a life of cushioned complacency. To the credit of his family, Roosevelt was brought up with appropriate levels of discipline and led a normal, happy childhood. His father became one of his idols later in life. He influenced a lot of Roosevelt's thinking, mannerisms, and the philosophies he adopted.

Roosevelt felt that for both the nation as well as the individual being, there was a need to combine certain qualities, in particular, efficiency and idealism. He believed that one could not thrive without the other. He believed in neither pacifism nor courage alone, quoting that *"love of peace is common among weak, short-sighted, timid, and lazy persons; and on the other hand, courage is found among many men of evil temper and bad character. Neither quality shall by itself avail".* To him, what was crucial was finding balance in everything. Justice and human progress could only result from the actions of brave men who chose the road to peace, regardless of what obstacles may have come in the way. This meant that the ideal man would have a nature that married peace to courage. It also meant that sometimes, they would have to do *what was right, regardless of whether the outcomes resulted in war or peace.*

Roosevelt was also a man of responsibility—someone who understood that modern society depended on the collective will of all, but that same collective will was subject to influence by each individual and their ability (or otherwise) to carry out their social and moral duties. He felt that duties needed to contribute to overall satisfaction in life, without which they would become mundane representations of obligations that no one could stick to in the long run.

Roosevelt appreciated generosity and humility. At the same time, he believed that just because people were gentle, they shouldn't "do nothing," as that would only make room for oppression and immorality. Gentleness had to be coupled with a side of fortitude, and people had to be willing to work for what they wanted. To him, *all for each and each for all* was a good enough quote to base a life on, but on the presupposition that every individual would work with a high level of determination and make the effort to not become an imposition on others. Without that, society would crumble.

Perhaps this was what formed the crux of the Roosevelt government. Theodore Roosevelt was a man of high ideals, and he sought to establish these ideals in the American people during his time as president. He understood that governments had the responsibility to ensure that the marginalized in a nation could survive on honest means and still have access to comforts, and the rich would do their part in contributing to the overall wellbeing of the society.

Life could be differently engineered for different people. What mattered to Roosevelt was the effort in ensuring there was justice in it for all.

To fully explore and understand the life and times of Theodore Roosevelt, this book has been divided into six chapters. The first will explore Roosevelt's early years and childhood; in particular, how he was seen as a frail child. The second chapter will dive into his education and early years in politics. This third chapter will then detail his transition from politician to the President of the United States.

The fourth chapter will highlight those events that occurred solely within the years of Roosevelt's presidency; while the fifth chapter will explore those events that happened after Theodore Roosevelt's presidency. This chapter will detail the supportive yet secret relationship with his cousin Franklin Delano Roosevelt. The sixth and final chapter of this book will talk about the legacy of Theodore Roosevelt, tackling the reputation he built for himself and how he is seen as one of the most powerful—and most vocal—presidents in United States history.

This book aims to provide a well-rounded and comprehensive look at the life, presidency, and influence of the 26th President of the United States.

To sit home, read one's favorite paper, and scoff at the misdeeds of the men who do things is easy, but it is markedly ineffective. It is what evil men count upon the good men's doing." —Theodore Roosevelt

***

Chapter One: Theodore Roosevelt's Childhood

"Courage is not having the strength to go on; it is going on when you don't have the strength." —Theodore Roosevelt

"I am a part of everything that I have read." —Theodore Roosevelt

"Knowing what's right doesn't mean much unless you do what's right." —Theodore Roosevelt

"You often hear people speaking as if life was like striving upward toward a mountain peak. That is not so. Life is as if you were traveling a ridge crest. You have the gulf of inefficiency on one side and the gulf of wickedness on the other, and it helps not to have avoided one gulf if you fall into the other." —Theodore Roosevelt

The Roosevelts raised their children to be hard-working, God-fearing men of the soil, rather than men of acclaim. Some of the family served in the Continental Army during the Revolution, but they received no awards. Likewise, though many of them were elected to Congress in the early years of the United States' nationhood, they did not have much of an impact.

From what we can tell, Theodore's grandparents had a very sizable sum to their name. His grandfather, Cornelius Van Schaack Roosevelt, was not only an entrepreneur who built upon his fortune but also an important socialite and philanthropist.

Cornelius's son Theodore—the father of the president, later known as Theodore Sr.—was born in 1831. He was a member of the plate-glass importing company Roosevelt & Son, working for the company's family branch. During the Civil War, Theodore Sr. was a passionate advocate for the Union. As one of the founders of the Union League Club, which was established to advocate for the Northern cause, he played a big role. During the war, it was he, William E. Dodge, Jr., and Theodore B. Bronson who developed the Allotment System, which provided soldiers' families with a steady income through military payroll deductions. He also contributed a great deal to charity in New York City. He was instrumental in establishing many New York landmarks, including the Metropolitan Museum of Art, the American Museum of Natural History, the New York Children's Orthopedic Hospital, and the New York City Children's Aid Society. To ensure his children valued discipline and obligation, he imposed his own energetic regard for such principles; but by all accounts, he was a good parent, and dearly loved by his children.

His mother, Martha Bulloch Roosevelt, was a socialite in the United States. Amongst her ancestors were Archibald Bulloch, William Bellinger Bulloch, and General Daniel Stewart.

"Teddy" Roosevelt (as he would famously come to be known) was born on October 27th, 1868, at number 28 on East 28th Street in New York City. By his own account, his house was furnished in a very conservative fashion, with furnishing that could only be described as severe. He has recounted that the furniture in the dining room was "so ferocious that it would scratch the children's legs when they sat down".

They also had a library with tables, chests, and bookcases which all looked very typical of a conventional American household. Roosevelt and the other children had a particular attachment to the house parlor, which was splendid to behold. Perhaps part of the reason behind this attraction was that it wasn't easily accessible. They could enter this parlor only on Sundays or on special occasions like parties.

At one point, Roosevelt and his brothers were brought to their grandfather's mansion on Fourteenth Street and Broadway, on the corner of Union Square. It was an enormous home for New York at the time. In the center of the hall there was a long room that rose to the ceiling; black-and-white tessellated marble tiles covered the floor, and an ornate staircase connected the upper level to the lower floor of the building. The kids couldn't get enough of the mosaic and spiral staircase in the foyer. Roosevelt had a real appreciation for home design, and that could be seen as early as his obsession with household items.

Summers were spent in the country—and how much the kids enjoyed them! The country was full of various kinds of creatures, including cats, dogs, bunnies, a raccoon, and a sorrel Shetland pony called General Grant. In the country, the children wandered around the woods with their bare feet, exploring, doing chores, and enjoying time with the other children in the neighboring houses.

Teddy adored Christmas, and it was an uplifting time for the entire household. Their stockings were hung at night, and the next morning they would race into their parents' bedroom, awaiting their gifts. The biggest presents, all those for individual children, were placed in the drawing-room, where the doors remained open until breakfast. Teddy would later try to make his own children's Christmases just as special.

Roosevelt was a happy child, albeit physically ill due to a tough run with asthma. He overcame this by embracing a lifestyle that taught him to deal with hardships.

He had a normal interest in objects around the house, though a few ornaments caught his fancy. One of these was a chandelier that was decorated with beautiful prisms, which he found very appealing. One day, he observed one of these baubles fall from the chandelier. He took it for himself and hid it in secret. He was afraid of being caught and punished, however, for having committed something that was, in his youthful eyes, a crime.

Teddy's connection with his father would prove to be very important to the future president. Theodore Sr. was his idol growing up. The elder Theodore was both physically strong and emotionally sensitive. He had no patience for greed, brutality, sloth, cowardice, or dishonesty. As the children grew older, he spent time helping them understand that men and women were held to the same standards of clean living.

Teddy was not so much in fear of his father as he was in awe of him. Theodore Sr. used tough love in the most understanding, sympathetic, and kind way. By Teddy's own testimony, his father was the only man he ever feared, though the man never physically punished Teddy, save on one occasion.

When Teddy was four, he bit his sister's arm. He immediately knew he had committed a grave offense. In fear of being punished, he ran into the kitchen, and hid under the kitchen table. Shortly thereafter, his father came inside the house from the yard and called out to him. The kind Irish chef knew he was under the table and didn't want to give him away. Instead, she looked beneath the table as if she did not know he was there. His father, catching onto the ruse, dropped to all fours and, upon seeing Teddy, gave chase as Teddy ran away. He was eventually caught, of course, and his punishment was fitting for the crime: all his privileges were revoked for a while, and he received a harsh talking to. This one event remained engraved in Teddy's mind.

In the next chapter, we will be moving on to the early academic and political life of Theodore Roosevelt. However, these stories of his early life are evidence that great people come from a variety of different backgrounds and childhoods like everyone else. Often, the distinguishing factor is how hard they are willing to work for what they believe in, as you will see going forward.

"Peace is normally a great good, and normally it coincides with righteousness, but it is righteousness and not peace which should bind the conscience of a nation as it should bind the conscience of an individual; and neither a nation nor an individual can surrender conscience to another's keeping." —
Theodore Roosevelt

***

Chapter Two: Education and Early Political Career

"A soft, easy life is not worth living, if it impairs the fiber of brain and heart and muscle. We must dare to be great; and we must realize that greatness is the fruit of toil and sacrifice and high courage... For us is the life of action, of strenuous performance of duty; let us live in the harness, striving mightily; let us rather run the risk of wearing out than rusting out." —Theodore Roosevelt

The Difficult Road of Education

Teddy's childhood was not without its hardships. In spite of his poor eyesight and many asthmatic episodes, the young Theodore dedicated his life to studying. He read on a wide variety of topics, anything from children's periodicals to poetry to novels by western writer Mayne Reid. He was just eight years old when he created the Roosevelt Museum of Natural History in his family's house and filled it with samples of his animal finds. He gathered things like bird and snake skins, the skull of a seal, and other various memorabilia, which he lovingly categorized and labeled.

The physical strength Roosevelt gained from exercising and building his body during his childhood was not enough to get him into Harvard, so he needed to improve himself to reach his objective. Over hours of weightlifting, calisthenics, and boxing, he worked through his physical weaknesses. He received an immense amount of support from his father during this period.

Theodore had a wealth of expertise, but his inability to handle the parts of the admission test that focused on algebra, Latin, and Greek, as opposed to other subjects, made him unappealing to Harvard. Working under a tutor called Arthur Cutler, he studied diligently for two years, and after passing the test, he entered Harvard. His dislike of drunkenness, his New York background, and his intelligence all distanced him from other Harvard men who were from prominent New England families and tended to have freewheeling attitudes.

Determined to succeed on all fronts of college life, he rose to the challenge and was reluctantly accepted into many prestigious Harvard societies, including the Porcellians. He did better than expected in his classes and got a Phi Beta Kappa key. While he did receive a general education at Harvard, it appears as though his studies had little impact when it came to real, earthbound politics.

Roosevelt was a very grounded man. He attended Columbia Law School after graduating from Harvard, as a legal background was crucial to his chosen vocation. It was taxing, but even as a fatigued law student, he went on to write a book about the War of 1812. After one semester, however, he decided that law was not the right path for him.

Early Politics and Personal Tragedy

Theodore first sought political position in 1881 when, wanting to serve the public, he tried to get elected to the New York State Assembly. Despite his failure, he tried again the following year, and won. He would be elected again in 1883.

After his victory in the general election of January 1882, he represented the twenty-first district of Manhattan in the state assembly. The first thing he did as a candidate was send an uninteresting introductory letter to his district's constituents. At this time, he was still a novice in the field of politics. There was no information on his credentials, opinions, or plans for what he would do if elected.

However, what he did have was the support of the majority. People loved him, and they stood behind his ideals. This was crucial to him getting elected as a minority leader in the state legislature.

Roosevelt was a Republican and was dismissed from his brief tenure as minority leader because of his independent thinking, reform-minded views, and refusal to recognize party bosses, yet his impact within the Assembly did not diminish. He got closer to Governor Grover Cleveland, a Democrat, with whom he started working. He was also introduced to Ansley Wilcox at this point. Governor Cleveland picked both of them to serve on a restoration committee that would work on restoring the natural beauty of the region around the Niagara Falls, New York.

The "Fifth Avenue Crowd," which included reputable people such as merchants, authors, bankers, and other members of high society, assisted in his election to the New York State Legislature, by helping him recruit prominent families in the area to support him. The members' remarks included that he was the right guy for the position, and that he was someone who had character and integrity. Teddy's advisers also urged him to do a saloon tour, which they quickly realized was a bad idea, due to his open nature. However, he was ultimately elected by almost 1,500 votes in total.

Things went smoothly for a while. In February 1884, however, tragedy struck. As he was working in the New York state legislature, attempting to enact legislation aimed at reforming the federal government, Roosevelt received a call from his family. When he came home, he discovered that his mother, Mittie, had died as a result of typhoid sickness. Later that same day, Bright's disease—a severe kidney ailment—took his wife, Alice Lee, whom he had married four years prior. They were deeply in love. Alice Lee had given birth to the couple's only child, daughter Alice, just two days before.

Roosevelt was heartbroken by the double catastrophe. He instructed others in his immediate vicinity not to mention his wife's name. He renounced office and left the infant Alice in the care of his sister Bamie, setting out for the Dakota territories at the end of 1884, where he lived as a rancher and served as sheriff for two years. When he wasn't busy herding cattle or serving as a local law enforcement officer, Roosevelt made time to satisfy his interest in history by reading and writing about it.

After a blizzard decimated his beloved herd of cattle in 1885, Roosevelt made the decision to return to the upper classes of eastern society. Upon returning to New York in 1886, he took on the responsibility of rearing his young daughter and entered politics once more.

Teddy decided to run for mayor of New York City in 1886. Though he hated the idea of running for that particular office, he decided to participate in the campaign to support the Republican Party. He also understood that his chances of winning were low. Henry George, an independent social reformer, was running against Abram Hewitt, the Tammany Hall-supported candidate. Both were formidable parties with years of experience in local politics. *"I'm just hoping for a good run,"* he said to a close friend.

In December 1886, he tied the knot with Edith Kermit Carow, a girl with whom he had been in love since childhood. Despite the loss of the mayoral race, the results of the campaign and new love provided him the boost of confidence he needed to return to politics sooner than he had previously planned. In 1889, Teddy Roosevelt became the Civil Service Commissioner under the office of President Benjamin Harrison, serving until 1895, when he rose to the office of the New York City police commissioner in 1895.

The Rough Riders

Then, in 1897, President McKinley appointed him to the office of the assistant secretary for the Naval Command, but he would not stay in this post long. In 1898, only a year after his appointment, Roosevelt joined the war effort against Spain. Always a man driven by his morals, Roosevelt felt that it would be correct to resign from his post and to represent his nation in war.

To do this, he formed a Volunteer Regiment which was composed of cowboys and adventurers—people from both the west and the east of America—who would go down in American lore as Roosevelt's Rough Riders. While the Spanish-American war was not a prolonged one, it was long enough for the Rough Riders to make their place in history. Roosevelt himself led this Regiment to success in the battle of San Juan Hill, their ride into glory. By the time he returned to the United States, he was a hero of the nation.

Following the conclusion of the Spanish-American War in 1898, Roosevelt was appointed governor of New York. Two years later, tired of Roosevelt's zeal and independence, New York Republicans organized for his selection as William McKinley's vice-presidential candidate, despite Roosevelt's opposition. They predicted that the vice presidency would bring his political career to a close in innocuous obscurity. A stroke of fate, however, would seal off this possibility forever. In 1901, President William McKinley, 25th President of the United States, was assassinated, propelling Roosevelt to the highest position in the land.

"Much has been given us, and much will rightfully be expected from us. We have duties to others and duties to ourselves; and we can shirk neither. We have become a great nation, forced by the fact of its greatness into relations with the other nations of the earth, and we must behave as beseems a people with such responsibilities." —Theodore Roosevelt

***

Chapter Three: Years Leading to Roosevelt Becoming the President

"I don't pity any man who does hard work worth doing. I admire him. I pity the creature who does not work, at whichever end of the social scale he may regard himself as being." —Theodore Roosevelt

Appointment as Governor of New York

At the dawn of 1898, the Republican Party of New York was on the hunt for a candidate to run for the post of Governor. One must remember that, at the time, the Republican administration was not doing too well. It was facing backlash from a number of political scandals and was subject to the critical scrutiny of the public eye. An urgent pick-me-up was needed to ensure that the Republicans would continue to be in power and could counter the growing popularity of the Democrats. They desperately needed someone who was loved and respected in the public eye, and who had established a name for himself as a lover and practitioner of clean government tactics.

Roosevelt had just returned from his highly successful stint in Cuba. However, Roosevelt was not so sure that this was the right professional calling for him. In addition, the Republicans faced some opposition from the party member who singularly claimed the most influence—Senator Thomas Platt—who, by all accounts, was an old-fashioned man who believed that one had to go through all the ranks in a party before they could lay claim to any electoral position. Platt was so powerful that the decision as to who the state convention would nominate for the post of governor was solely in his hands. He was not very keen on Roosevelt and was suspicious of the latter's progressive stance on reform, his disbelief in the conventional operation of institutional politics, and his massive popular following. He was worried that Roosevelt would turn out to be a challenge to his authority.

Platt regarded certain things as positives, however: Roosevelt was regular in terms of his showing up to support the Republican Party, and he was ardent in his criticism of the Democrats. Platt also figured that Roosevelt could be the only solution at hand to keep the Republicans at the helm of political affairs and in office, and this was by far more important than his personal misgivings.

So, in September 1898, Roosevelt attended a personal meeting with Platt in the senator's apartment situated at the Fifth Avenue Hotel. The people who believed in Roosevelt were worried that he was colluding with someone who was far too conservative. The reformers were convinced that to achieve anything, progressive reform was the call of the hour, something that was in no way possible around someone as conventional as Platt. But Roosevelt was someone who was governed by the dictates of pragmatic reasoning. He knew that if he came to office, he could work on the changes he wanted gradually. He was not interested in bringing down the system. Rather, he wanted to *reform it from within.* To do this, he needed to be in a higher office. So, he reached an agreement with Platt, and the latter agreed to his nomination, subject to always being consulted on matters of policy and practice.

Roosevelt based his political campaign on the simple promise of keeping a clean administration, and he relied on the public image he'd built to rise to the forefront. He was elected Governor of New York in 1898. He was not interested, however, in just being a simple "housekeeper" when it came to running the office of the Governor. While he was unsure of what he precisely wanted, one thing remained steadfast: he was going to initiate progressive reform.

It became increasingly apparent that the relationship between Roosevelt and Platt would be subject to a level of discord. They did not agree on a number of issues, most important among them being that Roosevelt did not adhere to Platt's definition of mutual discussion before coming to any final decisions on important appointments. One of Roosevelt's earliest decisions was the appointment of an administrator to oversee the running of the state canal system. This was an office that had been subject to a lot of scandal and public criticism during the run of the previous administration. Now, Platt wanted this post to go to a man by the name of Francis J. Hendricks. Roosevelt categorically opposed this—mostly because Hendricks was conservative and did not appreciate or want any progressive reform.

They reached a point of agreement when Roosevelt made a list of meritorious party men for the post and allowed Platt to choose a name from them. However, while this practice achieved peace, it also gave rise to a growing suspicion in Platt's mind that Roosevelt was, on all counts, an independent man.

This independence became a point of contention when it came to policy. Roosevelt was in favor of legislation that would allow the state supreme courts to go over the documents and accounts of corporations. He publicly showed his disfavor of monopoly legislation. He voraciously pushed for reforms in civil laws, including 8-hour workdays for employees of public offices and a minimum wages rule for teachers in the schools of New York City.

While all of these were against what Platt stood for, what got to him the most was Roosevelt's unequivocal support of taxing public franchises. This was loathed by New York's public corporations, many of whom were financing Platt's political regime. The bosses of the corporations made their displeasure known to Platt, who began to be afraid that he was losing his hold on the party because of his lack of control over the governor and his impetuous policies.

This was a delicate situation. While Roosevelt had begun offending the bigshots in the political field of New York City, he was still adored by the common people. This popularity also made him what he was at that stage: an efficient governor.

Roosevelt was very well aware of the hold he had on the imagination of the people. He made good use of the love they had for him to constantly push for his reformative programs. He held regular press conferences and conferred with subject experts on all manners of complex issues. Forever a man of the soil, he knew that to be powerful, he needed the will of the people by his side. Because of this, both the media and the public—two of the most important channels of political progress—supported him. So, in this atmosphere of public adoration, who would be willing to challenge the authority he posed?

Running For Vice President

As a highly successful "People's" Governor of New York, many of Roosevelt's supporters and admirers felt that the next logical step for him would be to take a step towards the presidency. Platt himself had considered this when he was deciding whether he should endorse Roosevelt for the post of Governor. He was afraid that given Roosevelt's magnetic charm and electric personality, he would naturally be a fit to run for the office of president. It was an eventuality he was dreading.

In 1900, the Republicans had already focused on William McKinley as the potential candidate for the office of the presidency. There was an underlying belief that Roosevelt would be a candidate in 1904. What would he do, however, once his office as Governor was completed in 1902 and he had two whole years at his disposal? The solution seemed to lie in making him the running mate to McKinley for the office of vice president.

Now, there are some debates as to why Roosevelt accepted the candidacy of the vice president, which at the time was generally regarded as an office of easy comfort and little duty. Surely, he was meant for greater things. One side of the debate is that his opponents in the Republican party felt that this would be a good way to cash in on his public popularity, while also retiring him from the limelight. *Two birds with one stone.* The other side of the debate, however, is that even his dear friends, people like Massachusetts Senator Henry Cabot Lodge, felt that he would be a good fit for this post simply because they knew that he would just use it as a steppingstone to greater heights. There was also the notion that functioning as the vice president and as the presiding Senate officer would allow Roosevelt to remain in the adoring eye of the public for far longer than his current position as the governor. Many of his western supporters also wanted him to run for office because they idolized him for the role he had played in the war.

As previously mentioned, Roosevelt did not look forward to the idea of becoming the vice president. To him, the position represented a shackle, something that would tether him and hinder his desire to bring about positive change. He was a man who thrived on work and being out in the field. A post of such languishment was obviously repellent to his very nature. As vice president, he would have little to zero executive responsibilities, and his voice would also be trampled on. To him, his work as a Governor was more vitalizing and stimulating.

It should also be mentioned that he did not appreciate the idea of presiding over the Senate. It was a task that he perceived as boring and mundane. His very righteous nature was in conflict with the idea of sitting still and listening to politicians who he disregarded in the highest aspect. To top it off, the office of the vice president ran on a lot of show and splendor. He had to have a social presence which mandated spending copious sums of money in entertaining big society names. This was, by all means, against the very core of Roosevelt's socially modest nature. As it lacked the opportunity to do anything constructive, the office of vice president was far off from what he wanted. He felt he made far better sense as secretary of war, but President McKinley already had someone else (Elihu Root) in mind for this. His next best choice was to be appointed as governor general of the Philippines, but his impetuous nature was not likely to do him any favors in this post.

Ultimately, it was Platt who stepped in to call the shots.

By this time, Platt was naturally on the hunt for a legitimate way to dethrone Roosevelt from his office as the governor of New York City. He decided that if he could lurch Roosevelt into a position that was all name and no power, he would effectively silence the voice of the budding reformer, gain back the support of the powerful corporations, and leave the room open for a subsequent candidate that he could manipulate. *Oh, how little was he aware of what would happen!*

While this agitation continued, and friends and foes alike continued to endorse Roosevelt's candidacy for the office of the vice president, McKinley kept his distance. He was not someone who was drawn to Roosevelt, in terms of either his personality or his stance on matters of policy. However, he also did not actively endorse anyone else as his running mate. At this point, the Republican leaders had become convinced that Roosevelt would bring glamor to the office of the vice president with his eccentric nature. He was the stuff of classic tales—a war hero, a man of the nation revered by his people. So, with no visible opposition, the eventuality that Roosevelt would become his running mate became more and more likely.

So, during the election of 1900, while Roosevelt was still opposed to the idea of becoming vice president, his very personality pushed him to the limelight naturally. His workaholic nature necessitated his presence in the convention, which enthused his party members to the point of a frenzy. Forever a man of impeccable taste, he showed up to the opening session wearing a black hat which bore a resemblance to the hat he wore during the Rough Rider's Cuban campaign, tying him to the one incident that had forever made him a hero in the eyes of the people. His nomination was signed, sealed, and delivered.

If nothing else, Roosevelt was a man grounded to his reality. He keenly understood that running for a second term as governor would be far more difficult than the first, particularly considering Platt's vocal disapproval of him. He also knew that powerful corporate entities now wanted him out of office. Gradually, he became convinced that perhaps this solution was the best for all parties involved. So, while he did not actively run for the office of vice president, once it was understood that this would be pushed upon him, he accepted it gracefully, with the singular determination to do the best he could in the given circumstances.

The Vice Presidency

While Roosevelt was not thrilled to be vice president, he was proud of his contribution to the ticket's win. Still, early on, he exhibited signs of dissatisfaction and passivity. His tendency towards decisive speech and action would return soon enough, but this early reluctance mirrored Roosevelt's unease in his new position. Accustomed to the forceful conduct of his own initiatives, he had to be vigilant not to alienate his chairman or the conservative establishment. For an energetic and unrestrained young man, this was a difficult situation.

The Senate assembled in a parliamentary session for four days beginning March 4th, led by the incumbent vice president, whose first task was always to preside over the Senate. Roosevelt had had four days to leave an impact during this brief tour, and according to all who observed him, he failed horribly. He proved to be as unsuitable for the role as he was so disinterested in it. His mind was wandering, and he only had a vague knowledge of Senate procedures. He considered himself to be the least productive Senate presiding officer the Senate had seen in a while. It was perhaps the one thing upon which they all could agree.

After the Senate recessed for the summer, Roosevelt returned to his home in New York to spend time with the family. He had married his childhood sweetheart, Edith Carow, two years after the death of his first wife. Edith was a reticent woman who never seemed to be comfortable with the attention paid to her husband and his career pursuits. In privacy, however, she had influence that reached far beyond the difficult task of raising the Roosevelt children, and also had a background role in many of Roosevelt's political decisions.

Vice President Roosevelt's professional obligations were restricted, at least for the time being, because President

McKinley did not consult him on strategy or selections. Although Vice President Hobart had been employed by McKinley in communication with the Senate, Roosevelt was ill-adapted for this job since he was more a public voice than a parliamentary operator. Furthermore, the Senate was led by Old Guard Republicans, the bulk of whom were apprehensive of Roosevelt's rambunctious inclinations. In any case, McKinley was unlikely to assign legislative responsibilities to his headstrong vice president because he denounced the younger man's lack of restraint. Roosevelt, likewise, resented McKinley's delay in dealing with sensitive matters. Whilst the two men's relationship was cordial, they were not intimate.

Thankfully for Roosevelt, some things panned out in his favor.

In the warmer months of 1900, Roosevelt began looking for alternative activities to fill the hole left by his indifference to his new position's official tasks. He resumed his regularly scheduled speaking engagements. He spoke to multitudes about the significance of having a strong fleet, as well as the threat posed by an increasingly powerful Germany. This demonstrated that, in the dearth of more serious matters, his thoughts were progressively drifting to one of his favorite subjects: international relations. Perhaps Roosevelt saw this as an area where he would have some leeway, considering that he and McKinley, although not always in complete accord on foreign policy, shared a lot of opinions. In this case, Roosevelt's harsher criticisms were directed at anti-imperialist Democrats, who also were McKinley's ideological enemies at the time.

The general political game plan of the Republicans at this time was to let McKinley host powerful guests and political authorities, which he did from his station in the White House. Meanwhile, Roosevelt was left to do the backend work on campaigns—something that suited his vigorous nature quite well. It gave him room to conduct political tours in the Midwest and the West, and to debate with the Democratic presidential candidate (W. J. Bryan) on issues like running the political field of the USA and tariffs. During this time, Roosevelt covered over twenty-one thousand miles, traveled to twenty-four states, and gave more than six hundred speeches. This added vitality to the Republican campaign. Essentially, the vice-presidential incumbent did the vital work, while the presidential candidate entertained.

Roosevelt also used the post to travel and show his vitality on a national scale. It was quickly discovered that he not only commanded the people of New York, but that his personality was magnetic regardless of where he went. It was a new era for campaign techniques—with increased emphasis on direct, personal methods for reaching out to people—and it was Roosevelt who brought this into the spotlight. Rather than just relying on the power of his party, he used mass media and public popularity tactics to directly communicate with the voters. He relied on public appreciation and righteousness to push for necessary reforms. By doing so, he was leading the way for an era of change in the American political campaigning environment.

The media also played a significant role in keeping Roosevelt in the limelight. To them, he was an interesting and unique political figure, someone who merited being written about. Roosevelt also had a lasting rapport with reporters, and while other politicians would only reach out to the press with mundane opinions of policy, Roosevelt gave them bits of himself: stories, anecdotes, and information that showed just how vibrant he was.

In 1904 he devoted considerable effort garnering support for the 1904 presidential election. Despite his fears that he would be denied the candidacy by the Democratic Party in New York, he cautiously adopted a route that would allow him to create a foundation of popular support. He concentrated his energies in the West, where he already had a solid support base.

Then came 1901, the year that changed everything.

President McKinley, a long-standing defender of protective tariffs, presented a significant policy address at the Pan American Exposition in Buffalo, New York, on September 5th. In his speech, the POTUS called for the creation of an era of mutual trade in which ancient trade barriers would have to be abolished. The president hosted a reception inside the Temple of Music the next day. At around four in the afternoon, a young radical named

Leon Czolgosz shot the president. McKinley fought for his life for a whole week, but on September 14th, he succumbed with the words *"Nearer, My God, To Thee"* on his lips.

This news that President McKinley had been shot brought Roosevelt back to Buffalo on the fourteenth of September. By the time he arrived, however, the president had already passed. After paying his respects, Roosevelt met with the cabinet and confirmed that he wished to continue in the shoes of McKinley and to strive for peace, prosperity, and honor of the United States as president. At forty-two, Theodore Roosevelt Jr. became the youngest president in the history of the United States.

"I cannot consent to take the position that the door of hope— the door of opportunity—is to be shut upon any man, no matter how worthy, purely upon the grounds of race or color. Such an attitude would, according to my convictions, be fundamentally wrong." —Theodore Roosevelt

Chapter Four: The Presidency of Theodore Roosevelt

"Unless a man is master of his soul, all other kinds of mastery amount to little." —Theodore Roosevelt

Roosevelt's promise to carry on McKinley's principles was not only intended to calm the country, but it was also compatible with his view of the vice president's position in the administration. Roosevelt, while police commissioner of New York City a few years prior, had classified the office of the vice president as a functionless one, save for the potential of the incumbent to later on become the leader of the whole country. Accordingly, he stressed that the vice president should, to the greatest extent possible, represent the same perspectives and principles that have secured the confirmation vote and appointment of the president, and that he should be a man who is well-regarded in the party's councils, respected by his compatriots and party leaders, and capable of taking over the work of his chief in the event that the latter should be killed or otherwise incapacitated in the course of his duties.

Without a doubt, the individual who held the position in September 1901 did not correspond to this paradigm. For a while, perhaps conventional wisdom prevailed, and Roosevelt felt that he had to follow in the previous president's footsteps.

But, as the time to be in office approached, he understood that the *people and the officials wanted him in his own capacity— they wanted Theodore Roosevelt, not the successor of McKinley.* Roosevelt had not been given the position of the president because of his resemblance to McKinley, and now that he was in the White House, he would not hesitate to go his own route.

His first annual address to Congress, in which he called for some kind of corporate control, served as a warning that American society with Roosevelt would indeed be distinctly different from what it was under McKinley's administration. Roosevelt started pursuing an environment protection project immediately, and within a few months, he was bringing an antitrust lawsuit against Northern Securities Company in federal court. He would make a real effort to navigate a moderate route in between the Old Guard and the revolutionary Republicans. But the demand for change was mounting, and Roosevelt's sympathies were always with the reformers.

President Roosevelt had received a series of benefits from his previous incumbent. First, Roosevelt inherited a strong and effective party structure, which had been created by Mark Hanna and which he immediately started to transform into his own. He made good use of all positions and ties he had previously established to empower his followers and make preparations for the general elections of 1904, which took place in Chicago. He also inherited a competent and capable cabinet. He would place a tremendous amount of reliance on individuals such as U.S. Secretary of State Hay, Secretary of War Elihu Root, and McKinley's private secretary George Cortelyou, among others. Roosevelt had also gained valuable experience from McKinley's White House staff in the area of public relations. The McKinley administration, largely as a result of the foresight of Cortelyou, had instituted a number of novel approaches to dealing with the press. It was the first time a president had employed press statements, pre-released speech transcripts, and "test blimps" to influence news coverage. Roosevelt used this efficiency in conjunction with his own enormous personality to control the news media. His ability to control his own publicity through his control over the material that was published in the newspapers was remarkable.

With the vigorous nationwide program Roosevelt initiated as the vice president, Roosevelt had disregarded conventional wisdom and showed his ability to promote the Republican cause and communicate to people in a manner that McKinley had failed to do. McKinley, who had been well aware of the media's influence, may have used Roosevelt expressly for this role, as a kind of "public persuader" for the government. McKinley had previously said that he intended to seek trade reciprocity agreements during his second term, that he had started to draft an antitrust agenda, and that he may take up the tariff problem during his second term, among other things. Roosevelt was now the best person to sell these initiatives to the general people.

Because Roosevelt served as vice president for such a short period of time, he'd had little influence on the position while in office. However, Roosevelt still left a significant effect on the office because of this talent for public relations, popularizing it and making it more accessible to the American people.

Roosevelt's domestic policy—known as the "Square Deal"—included a pledge to fight huge manufacturing mergers, or trusts, that threatened to restrict commerce. In 1902, his administration was successful in bringing a complaint under the Sherman Antitrust Act against the Northern Securities Company, a railroad conglomerate established by James J. Hill, E.H. Harriman, and J.P. Morgan that had previously been declared ineffectual by the Supreme Court. His intervention in a lengthy coal strike in Pennsylvania the following year, employing a mix of negotiating techniques, brought the strike to a stop and resulted in a small wage rise for the striking workers.

Roosevelt also employed his administrative authority to promote his commitment to environmental protection. The passage of the National Reclamation Act (committed to vast irrigation initiatives in the American West) in June 1902 marked the beginning of his presidency's first significant legislative accomplishment. Furthermore, Roosevelt set aside over 200 million acres for national forests, reserves, and wildlife refuges, nearly five times the total amount of land set aside by all of his predecessors combined. His support for the displacement of numerous Native Americans from their native lands, including the transfer of roughly 86 million acres of tribal land to the national forest system, was a key element of that process.

His presidency infused legitimacy into the progressive movement, bringing the authority of the White House to bear on welfare legislation, regulatory measures, and the preservation movement, among other things. Many aspects of Roosevelt's policy were motivated by a desire to make society more inclusive, while also providing economic opportunities for all Americans.

The relationship between the government and large businesses was also altered by the president. The government had usually granted unlimited powers to the giants of business to achieve their objectives prior to his election. During his presidency, Roosevelt felt that the government should have the authority and duty to control large enterprises to ensure that its activities would not have a detrimental impact on the general population. Although he never questioned the legitimacy of big business, he did believe that its presence represented a natural phase in the country's economic development.

Foreign relations were also transformed under Roosevelt's leadership. He believed that the United States had a worldwide duty and that a robust foreign policy benefited the nation's national interest. He jumped into Latin America with little hesitancy, supervising the Panama Canal talks on behalf of the United States and intervening in Venezuela and the Dominican

Republic to maintain peace in the area. He also pushed Congress to build the United States Navy, which he thought would prevent prospective adversaries from attacking the nation. He also devoted his time and energy to negotiating peace accords, with the goal of achieving a more equitable distribution of power around the globe.

During his presidency, Theodore Roosevelt established himself as one of the most active and beloved presidents in the country, easily gaining reelection in 1904. The Hepburn Act (which increased railroad regulation) and the Pure Food and Drug Acts were among the major pieces of domestic legislation he championed, and he was instrumental in bringing the United States into a more prominent position in international affairs. For his efforts in mediating the Russo-Japanese War, he was awarded the Nobel Peace Prize in 1906, making him the very first American to be given the prestigious award.

Even after leaving office, Roosevelt actively campaigned for the causes that he believed in. In 1912, the Progressive Party's New Nationalism began a campaign for protective federal regulation that foreshadowed the progressive politics of the 1930s and those that would follow a generation later in the 1960s. To be sure, Roosevelt's progressive platform included virtually every progressive goal that would eventually be codified into such landmark legislation as FDR's New Deal; Harry S. Truman's Fair

Deal; John F. Kennedy's New Frontier; and Lyndon B. Johnson's Great Society (among others).

In terms of political style, Roosevelt was the first president to bring the concept of "gravitas" into the legislative equation. He had a solid connection to the general populace and was well-versed in the art of using the media to influence public opinion. He was the very first president for whom the victory was decided more on the merits of the person than on the platform of the political party. When Americans voted Republican in 1904, they were primarily voting for Roosevelt the person rather than for him as the predefined candidate of the Republican Party. Roosevelt, known as "The People's President," leveraged his passion to win votes, influence change, and shape public opinion throughout his tenure in office. It was through this procedure that he altered the presidential office for good.

"It is not the critic who counts. ... The credit belongs to the man who is actually in the arena; whose face is marred by the dust and sweat and blood; who strives valiantly ... who, at worst, if he fails, at least fails while daring greatly; so that his place shall never be with those cold and timid souls who know neither victory or defeat." —Theodore Roosevelt

"Do what you can, with what you have, where you are." — Theodore Roosevelt

Chapter Five: Life Beyond the White House

"Our aim is not to do away with corporations; on the contrary, these big aggregations are an inevitable development of modern industrialism. ... We are not hostile to them; we are merely determined that they shall be so handled as to subserve the public good. We draw the line against misconduct, not against wealth." —Theodore Roosevelt

While in Congress and throughout his presidency, Roosevelt's ability to connect with the American people was incredibly valuable. It's hard to imagine any politician in American history with such a talent, much less someone of Roosevelt's prominence. It didn't matter who he was talking to; Theodore could persuade anyone that he was one of their own, stood up for their values, and was looking out for their interests above all else. During his time in office, he traveled extensively throughout the country on campaign trips to educate the world about his economic and diplomatic positions. He was a charismatic public speaker who, while speaking in front of a large crowd of people, would often expand his voice, without the assistance of a microphone, to the point of breaking it. His speeches were animated, full of vibrant gestures, and contained an electric air that roused his audience. This was the first time a president had addressed the American people in this manner, so it should come as no surprise that so many people turned out to hear him speak.

On a daring tour of the Midwest and New England in 1902, Roosevelt started campaigning for President of the United States. In the course of this trip, he spoke out against the burgeoning corporatocracy and powerful trusts, the trade with Cuba, taxes, as well as the situation in the Philippines, where a rebellion was taking place. While visiting Pittsfield, Massachusetts, Roosevelt's transport was hit by an electric trolley car, which caused him to lose consciousness. Roosevelt emerged from the hospital with a swollen face and an injured leg, but he continued the tour for the rest of the day, halting in Bridgeport, Connecticut, to communicate to a crowd of thirty thousand people before continuing on to New York City. While at first insisting that he was uninjured, he eventually agreed to have fluid drained from a blister that had developed on his leg, due to the urging of several foreign dignitaries who voiced their concern. His mobility was limited for several weeks while he was confined to a wheelchair.

Roosevelt made significant changes to daily life in the White House, both figurative and literal. During his administration, the eastern and western wings of the White House were built, resulting in a substantial increase in the total square footage of the building. In the course of his presidency, the First Family hosted a number of stylish and costly parties and social gatherings for members of the Washington elite. Alice's debut ball in 1902 was a glamorous affair, with all of Washington's young men and women in attendance, such as the child of a Russian noblewoman, the daughter of the British ambassador, and even Alice's distant cousin Franklin Delano Roosevelt, among others. Also hosted in the White House was Alice's marriage to Republican congressman Nicholas Longworth, which took place in 1906.

Less than a month after taking office, Roosevelt sparked outrage throughout the country when he asked Booker T. Washington to lunch with him at the White House. Washington, a former Southern slave who rose through the ranks to become a learned man and renowned professor at his alma mater, the Tuskegee Institute, was well-known across the country. The South was furious that Roosevelt had asked a black man to lunch with him, and many Northerners were conflicted about the invitation as well. Roosevelt reacted quickly, saying that the nation's outrage only demonstrated that he had made the right choice. In numerous letters, he further chastised the American people for making snap decisions based on their skin color.

The White House was never a haven of peace and quiet. The Roosevelt youngsters and their friends had a complete run of the building and quickly gained national notice for their attractiveness and the Roosevelt zest for life that was typical of the family. They were renowned as the "White House Gang" after the White House where they were stationed. America's fascination with the children was piqued by the two younger boys, Archie and Quentin, who were especially endearing. Newspapers all across the country carried articles about Quentin's many pranks and impersonations. Once, he snuck a pony through to the house, up the elevator, and into his brother's room. He was caught. In another instance, a group of congressmen were scared to death when Quentin placed a four-foot-long snake near his father's office, an act for which he later expressed regret.

Though burdened with the weight of the presidency, Roosevelt refused to let go of his passion for adventure, fitness, and pushing his own personal boundaries. A number of his own sporting activities, in fact, contributed to the commotion in the White House. Tennis was one of his greatest joys, which he enjoyed playing with the younger folk of his staff on a regular basis. In contrast to the elder members of Roosevelt's administration, these young men were known as his "Tennis Cabinet," a nickname given to them by the press. Roosevelt also loved horseback riding, rowing, trekking, and wood-chopping, and he devised a number of obstacle courses that required participants to traverse tough terrain in a short period of time. Indoor sports like martial arts, wrestling, and boxing were among his favorites to train in while at the White House. Theodore Roosevelt was blinded in his left eye after being struck in the left corner of the eye while sparring with a military companion in 1905. He didn't tell anybody about this, however, until almost 10 years later, in 1914, before having another surgery to repair the damage.

"No nation deserves to exist if it permits itself to lose the stern and virile virtues; and this without regard to whether the loss is due to the growth of a heartless and all-absorbing commercialism, to prolonged indulgence in luxury and soft, effortless ease, or to the deification of a warped and twisted sentimentality." —Theodore Roosevelt

"It is of little use for us to pay lip-loyalty to the mighty men of the past unless we sincerely endeavor to apply to the problems of the present precisely the qualities which in other crises enabled the men of that day to meet those crises." —Theodore Roosevelt

Chapter Six: The Legacy of Theodore Roosevelt

"When you play, play hard; when you work, don't play at all."
—Theodore Roosevelt

During his seven years as president, Roosevelt instituted a number of progressive policies that are still in effect in the United States today. As a precursor to the Federal Trade Commission, he established The Bureau of Corporations, which was an investigative entity that pursued antitrust violations against business interests. A far-stretch from the horrific meatpacking industry conditions at the time, Roosevelt's Pure Food and Drug Act, along with the Meat Inspection Act, brought about greater consumer safeguards and regulation for the meatpacking sector.

Using the cogent force of the United States military, Roosevelt said that the United States could maintain its dominance over strategically critical portions of the Western Hemisphere. Notwithstanding the fact that the United States employed military intervention in a variety of situations to achieve its goals, it lacked the power and willingness to impose its will militarily on the entire continent of South and Central America. Because of this, the United States employed informal means of empire to assert power over the hemisphere, such as 'money diplomacy', to establish dominance over the region.

The United States intervened in Latin America on a number of occasions under the presidentship of Roosevelt. It also maintained authority over Cuba and Puerto Rico throughout Roosevelt's presidency, and he committed naval forces to establish Panama's separation from Colombia in 1901 so as to attain a U.S. Canal Zone during his tenure. Roosevelt also issued the "Roosevelt Corollary" to the Monroe Doctrine in 1904, which declared the United States to have political discretion in the Caribbean. As President James Monroe stated in his annual speech to Congress in 1823, any military action in Latin America by a European nation would be viewed as a danger to American security. Franklin D. Roosevelt reaffirmed and expanded the Monroe Doctrine, proclaiming that the United States had the authority to intervene in any Latin American country to address administrative and fiscal problems.

Roosevelt's strategy justified many and repeated police actions by U.S. marines and naval troops in corrupt Caribbean and Latin American countries, and it made it possible for the United States to establish a naval facility in Cuba, which became known as Guantanamo Bay.

The Marine Corps occupied the Dominican Republic in 1905, and the United States government maintained financial supervision over all Dominican administration. Imperialists frequently presented such measures as being nearly humanitarian in nature. As enhanced adherents of nation-building and civilization, white Anglo-Saxon societies such as those economies of the United States as well as the British Empire were praised for their contributions to the uplifting of debtor nations in Latin America who lacked the uncompromising character traits of determination and self-regulation.

Roosevelt was not necessarily in favor of military expansion as a means of achieving his goals. As a matter of fact, the president was of the ardent belief that when dealing with Latin American countries, he was not looking for national glory or territorial expansion and felt war or involvement should only be used as a last resort for resolving issues with troublesome regimes. To Roosevelt, such activities were critical to maintain justice and tolerance in the world. When it came to protecting national interests and domains of influence, Roosevelt believed that military force should be used only in the most extreme circumstances. His belief that the American sphere covered not just Hawaii and also the Caribbean, as well as much of the Pacific, was also shared by other historians. At a time when Japanese triumphs over the Soviet Union endangered the situational power politics and balance of authorities, Roosevelt intervened, and achieved a place of peaceful diplomacy between all parties. In 1906, he was awarded the Nobel Peace Prize for his efforts in facilitating peace talks between Soviet and Japanese officials.

Roosevelt remained active in politics even after the end of his time in office, advocating for public policies that would form the foundation of the eventual federal government. These programs included old-age pensions, unemployment compensation, a progressive income tax, child labor restrictions, and the right for women to vote.

The conservation of the country's natural resources, and the establishment of resource protection as a mainstay of executive power, were perhaps his most celebrated achievements. The 1906 American Antiquities Act, which grants presidents the authority to protect public lands, was particularly significant. There are about two hundred and thirty million acres of government land that Theodore Roosevelt helped create during his presidency and which represents his protection legacy. Most of the area—over one hundred and fifty million acres—has been designated as national forests. In 1905, Roosevelt established the United States Forest Service (now known as the USFS), which is part of the Department of Agriculture. The objective was to protect woods so that they may be used in the future. Roosevelt was a staunch supporter of exploiting the nation's resources, but he was also concerned about ensuring the long-term viability of those resources.

Despite the pressures of structural transformation and hypercompetitive industrial interests, Roosevelt established the United States Forest Service and a slew of protected outdoor spaces, including a hundred and fifty national forests, fifty-one federal bird reserves, four national game preserves, five nature reserves, and eighteen national monuments, all through the Antiquities Act of 1906. Approximately two hundred and thirty million acres of public land were protected during Theodore Roosevelt's administration.

A conservative nation became a more progressive one under Theodore Roosevelt's leadership and went from being one that was intent on ruining its national environment to one that was beginning to conserve it. The United States went from being a weak and domestically focused government to one with imperialistic aspirations. The presidency, too, transformed, gaining more authority and becoming a public fascination as a result of these developments. Theodore Roosevelt's politics guided the United States of America into the twentieth century, and much of his work helped set the tone that would carry the United States through it.

Let's take a minute to go through all of Roosevelt's achievements, and one will see that he achieved a lot in a remarkably limited time frame:

- President Roosevelt operated in an open and transparent manner, with a clear goal in mind. First and foremost, he promised to enforce each law on the books, without making any exceptions in furtherance of any individual or entity; second, he suggested to Congress that new legislation be enacted to prevent further encroachment by capitalists in fields where they had already been checked; and third, he stressed the importance of Congress acting immediately to protect national resources that had been allowed to go to waste or had been seized and manipulated by private interests.

- Among the provisions of President Roosevelt's Square Deal were consumer protection, government supervision over huge enterprises, and biodiversity conservation. The purpose of the Square Deal would be to assist middle-class residents while also allowing businesses to operate without being subjected to the complex demands that were frequently made by labor movements. Roosevelt strongly believed that the authorities should interfere between giant corporations that were just interested in accumulating riches and cheating the people for their own gain.
- During his presidency, Roosevelt worked to get the *Newlands Reclamation Act* passed in 1902, which provided funds for irrigation projects around the country. In the beginning, it was limited to the first thirteen states, but as time went on, other states were added. The selling of moderately dry public land that had previously been

controlled by the government provided the necessary funds. Eventually, the Act spurred agriculture and altered many states in the West, converting previously unproductive territory into productive farmland and ranchland. Fruit and vegetable producers in states such as Arizona, Nevada, Oregon, and South Dakota have benefited from the Act, and the result is a diverse array of fruits, vegetables, and nuts.

- A piece of legislation known as the Elkins Act was approved in 1906 and was strongly associated with President Roosevelt's Square Deal. As a result of this Act, railways could no longer provide rebates to corporations they liked. Many smaller farmers were forced into positions where they did not have fair access to the locomotives and railway roads as a result of this action by the railroads. Roosevelt's Act put a stop to this.

- Later, the Hepburn Act was passed in reaction to widespread public outcry about unregulated rate rises. The Interstate Commerce Committee was also abolished, but federal rules over the railroad industry were increased as a result of the Act.

- In the locomotive and textile sectors, workers were frequently injured as a result of their jobs. Workers began to be injured in greater numbers as railroads grew and fabric factories became more plentiful as industrial work developed. Leading up to the FELA Act, which made employers accountable for workplace injuries, individuals would have to file a lawsuit to seek compensation for their losses. Despite the fact that workers still had to establish that their employer was irresponsible, the new regulations endorsed by President Roosevelt made it simpler for workers to be reimbursed when their employer was at fault.

- President Roosevelt was successful in keeping inflation at a low level both during his first and second terms, with the rate rising by only five percent during both of his terms. Historically, inflation in the single digits has been associated with strong, robust economic growth, and during his tenure as president, inflation averaged one percent each year on average.

- President Roosevelt was a staunch advocate in support of the construction of a canal that would connect the Pacific to the Atlantic Ocean by slicing through Panama. With a length of 48 miles, the segment runs through all of the Isthmus of Panama and has become an important contribution to international maritime trade. It was not until France attempted to build the canal that the concept of a feasible canal became a reality, despite the fact that it had been proposed as early as 1534. Despite the fact that

France was involved in the project, they were forced to abandon it due to a high death rate among the workers and a number of engineering problems. Roosevelt was successful in assuming control of the project in 1904, and the channel was finally completed in 1914. Approximately a thousand ships passed through the canal in its first year of operation.

- President Theodore Roosevelt had strong feelings towards the United States Navy during his tenure as Assistant Secretary of the Navy and during his presidency. The strength and power of the United States Navy were enhanced during those years, and the Great White Fleet was deployed around the world for more than a year to demonstrate America's newfound strength and naval capabilities. Despite the fact that the United States Fleet began with only 90 tiny ships, it swiftly developed into a surface fleet with a large number of combat vessels, largely because of Roosevelt's efforts.

- Theodore Roosevelt was an avid athlete and would have been the first individual in the United States to achieve the rank of brown belt in judo. He enjoyed a good fight and would often demonstrate his prowess during dinners with dignitaries of note in the community. He had mats installed in the White House, and he could often be spotted sparring with anyone who was willing to take up arms with him.

- In addition to being an environmentalist, President Roosevelt worked to conserve wilderness areas and wildlife populations. Established in 1905, the United States Forest Service is a federal agency that functions under the Department of Agriculture. One of his primary objectives in founding the USFS was to ensure the long-term viability of the country's natural resources. He intended to ensure that the forests would be around for future generations to enjoy, and his name is still associated with environmentalism and the beauty of American nature today.

"It is only through labor and painful effort, by grim energy and resolute courage, that we move on to better things." — Theodore Roosevelt

"People ask the difference between a leader and a boss. The leader leads, and the boss drives." —Theodore Roosevelt

Final Words

"It is a bad thing for a nation to raise and to admire a false standard of success; and there can be no falser standard than that set by the deification of material well-being in and for itself." —Theodore Roosevelt

We have reached the conclusion of this book, so allow me to begin this last chapter with a topic that is quite personal to me: what is it about a specific person's persona that makes it irresistible?

For the most part, we are looking for someone who makes us feel secure and self-confident. It is important for us to believe that our leaders are capable of making difficult decisions and of caring for us no matter what obstacles may arise. The captivating personalities of others, the individuals who demonstrate their concern not just through their words but also by their actions and choices, capture our attention. We are looking for someone who is not scared, who is just, and who is unbiased. Teddy Roosevelt embodied all of these characteristics, which were tied together in a captivating mix.

Teddy Roosevelt may have been born in a stable household, but his childhood was far from easy. Growing up, he was a slender, frail young boy, and his battle with asthma was poised to make an invalid out of him at a particular point in time. Having been denied the opportunity to learn and develop with other boys his age, he became fearful when placed in situations where he could not confront others on an equivalent physical footing. And so, he followed his own desires with even more determination. He read a wide range of literature, some of which appeared to be beyond the comprehension of a little lad, yet he gained knowledge from each book. His ability to concentrate took his family by surprise.

I have often found that a literary mind is sensitive to people. When individuals read, we open ourselves to a host of emotions and become receptive to different world views. This makes readers interesting people. It is often thought that in a room of crowded people, no matter how dull the conversation is, a reader will always find a way to occupy the minds and imaginations of others.

Teddy's early childhood inculcated a rigorous sense of order and patience in him. This helped him to the end of his days. There were few other people with his ailment, and the zeal to still not give up, to continue on the course of rigorous, difficult exercises that would one day help him travel the whole country without falling sick. He could be a true people's man. Someone who always showed up.

A young Theodore went off on his own to join Harvard University in the fall of 1876. He excelled in his scientific courses while at

Harvard, but he ruled out science as a career option due to the need of functioning in an enclosed laboratory. The same year, Roosevelt encountered and actively pursued Alice Hathaway Lee. In his handwritten diary, Roosevelt expressed his feelings for her as being "truly in love." Losing Alice to an accident would derail him later on, but he would resurface like a Phoenix from the ashes of his sorrow.

When his mother and loving wife Alice both passed on the same day in 1884, he was heartbroken, and he was forced to become a single father to his daughter.

Why is this so important? It shows us his human nature, that he, like all of us, fell in love and married his soul mate, that he went through momentous loss—loss that can often destabilize the strongest among us, and he still emerged from all of it as a man of power. He changed education and career choices like a million of us. He had moments of doubt like we all do. *It was possible to both relate to and look up to him.* One of these traits in itself is wonderful, but both seal the deal to being respected and adored by people.

Because of the gravity of these tragedies, however, he did withdraw from public life for a while and took refuge in the Dakota badlands. While there, Roosevelt healed from disillusionment and bereavement for two years, while also developing lifelong connections that would later be beneficial to his political ambitions. It is widely believed that his commitment to conservation was cemented at his Elkhorn Ranch, where he grew more distressed about the endangerment and the destruction of their natural environments. Roosevelt acknowledged that these issues were caused by desertification of land, erosion, and other forms of land mismanagement. He made a promise to himself that he would take whatever measures necessary to preserve these natural riches.

Roosevelt maintains that close friends like Joe Murray did him a world of good. He understood the president and accepted the course of action with which he ran the government. His friends did not have any other desires save for Roosevelt to make a success of his time in office, and they supported his actions and directions with enthusiasm and uplifted him.

No one event had more of an impact on Theodore Roosevelt's career as a politician than William McKinley's death in September 1901. President Theodore Roosevelt assumed office at the age of forty-two, making him the youngest President of the United States of America before or since. Roosevelt's goal was to make democracy work for the public from the beginning, and the people had never had greater need for government than they had under Roosevelt. Because of the post-Civil War technological boom, the individuals who dominated industry and finance had amassed tremendous wealth and power in their hands. One of Roosevelt's main priorities would be the regulation of the big corporate trusts to promote fair competition while avoiding the socializing of the free enterprise system. His investigations included railways, laborers, and the packaged food sector, among other things. The restrictions he put in place were small by today's standards, but taken together, they represented a major first step in an era when cautionary banners and public lawsuits were common.

On the international stage, America was poised to take the reins of global leadership. The battle with Spain resulted in the possession of the Philippine Islands and the territory of Guam, extending the country's geographical boundaries nearly to the Asian continent. America's commercial and military concerns in the Far East, and also Central and South America, would only grow if the Panama Canal were built. In an era when oceanic steamship travel was becoming more popular, the country's feeling of isolation was on the brink of becoming as out of date as yardarms and sails.

Roosevelt was a conservative by inclination, yet he was contemporary in the manner he handled the nation's issues and contemporary in his approach to the office of president. According to him, if the citizens were to be represented, then it was the president's responsibility to coordinate the efforts that would be beneficial to them as well as the country. Since Abraham Lincoln and Jackson preceding him, no president has used his executive authority as a member of the same branch of government as the other branches of government. Roosevelt believed he was within his rights to use authority if the Law did not expressly prohibit the president from doing so.

In March 1903, he signed an executive order establishing one of fifty-one nationwide bird sanctuaries throughout the country. These, as well as the nature reserves and monuments he established, are part of his enduring legacy. Roosevelt was re-elected to a second term and then resigned from the presidency in 1909. After losing the presidency in 1912, Roosevelt ran as an outsider candidate for the Progressives (also known as Bull Moose) Party in an effort to reclaim the position. In Wisconsin, while giving a campaign speech, he was shot by a saloon-keeper because he didn't agree with his political views. President Roosevelt refused to travel to the infirmary until he had completed his address, which took more than an hour. Despite surviving the murder attempt, he was defeated in the presidential election by Woodrow Wilson.

Roosevelt used his retirement to go on vacation in Africa and explore the rainforests of Brazil, among other activities. Rarely has a president left and returned to the White House as president in American history. Theodore Roosevelt had loved his time as president just as much as any individual could have imagined. Filling the void left would need something monumental and spectacular, and Roosevelt prepared his near future with this in mind. The thought of a lengthy safari in Africa helped him to look forward to what would otherwise have been a gloomy scenario: his impending retirement.

Roosevelt, with the assistance of numerous British specialists, supervised every aspect of the preparations, including the route, equipment and clothes, food and supplies, weaponry, people, and expenditures. Since his childhood, he had been an ardent naturalist and hunter, and he continued to be so. His genuine interest in African fauna led him to plan a safari that was as scientific as conceivable, and he persuaded the Smithsonian to join him by offering to make significant contributions to the institution's fledgling collection of African wildlife specimens in exchange for the opportunity to travel with him. Kermit Roosevelt, Roosevelt's son, was asked to accompany him for companionship, provided the young man was prepared to miss his first year of college studies at Harvard. Kermit was already persuaded when he first heard of the plans.

You see, when people looked at him, they saw a leader, but they also saw a man who was *just like them*. A man who was a responsible parent and took his son on travels with him. A man who spent time with his family. Someone who took the time to go around the vast country and listen to everyone. Someone who balanced commerce with ecology. He was a tangible aspiration for people.

Ever the family man alongside his political affiliations, Roosevelt was deeply tied to all personal matters. His wife and children adored him, and it is said that his wife also had a major role in many of the decisions that sustained him. They were a model, happy family. However, after the loss of his youngest child, Quentin, during World War I, Roosevelt's health began to deteriorate. He passed away on January 6, 1919, the following year.

Theodore Roosevelt was the very first "inadvertent" president who went on to win an uncontested election for the presidency. His administration saw the expansion of the federal government's reach into sectors like industry, employment, the environment, and consumer protection, as well as international affairs, among other things. Many historians have referred to him as the first modern president, and he is widely regarded with love and respect.

"The unforgivable crime is soft hitting. Do not hit at all if it can be avoided; but never hit softly." —Theodore Roosevelt

Timeline Of Theodore Roosevelt

❖ **1858**

➢ On October 27th Theodore Roosevelt born to Theodore Sr. and Martha Roosevelt.

➢ He is their second child.

➢ The first child born before Theodore is a sister named Anna.

❖ **1860-1861**

➢ Theodore's two younger siblings Elliot and Corrine are born.

❖ **1870**

➢ Begins his love of physical fitness.

➢ Inspired by his father's work with the American Museum of Natural History; Theodore makes his own museum in his home – the Roosevelt Museum of Natural History.

➢ Visits Europe for the first time.

❖ **1872-1873**

➢ Second trip overseas; this time to Egypt and other Holy lands.

➢ Receives his first shotgun.

- ❖ **1876-77**
  - ➢ Begins his education at Harvard University in September.
  - ➢ That summer he writes "The Summer Birds of The Adirondacks."

- ❖ **1878**
  - ➢ His father, Theodore Sr, dies of stomach cancer.
  - ➢ Meets Alice Hathaway Lee.

- ❖ **1880**
  - ➢ Graduates Harvard.
  - ➢ Gets engaged to and marries Alice.
  - ➢ In the winter of that year, officially joins the Republican Party and begins Columbia Law School.

- ❖ **1881**
  - ➢ Climbs the Matterhorn.
  - ➢ Elected to the New York State Assembly.

- ❖ **1882-1883**
  - ➢ Publishes literary work *The Naval War of 1812*.
  - ➢ Becomes Second Lieutenant of the National Guard.
  - ➢ Elected Speaker of Republican Assembly.

❖ **1884**

- ➢ Has first child with Alice Lee Roosevelt.

- ➢ His mother Martha dies due to typhoid fever.

- ➢ Alice Lee dies, only hours after Martha, due to kidney failure.

- ➢ Establishes Elkhorn Ranch.

❖ **1885**

- ➢ Begins to court childhood sweetheart, Edith Carow.

❖ **1887**

- ➢ Has first son with Edith in the fall – Theodore Jr.

❖ **1888**

- ➢ Publishes *Essays in Practical Politics, Ranch Lie and the Hunting Trials,* and *Life of Gouverneur Morris*

❖ **1889**

- ➢ Has second son with Edith – Kermit.

- ➢ Publishes *The Winning of the West.*

- ➢ Starts as U.S Civil Service Commissioner in Washington D.C.

- ❖ **1891**
  - ➤ Has another child with Edith – a daughter named Ethel.

- ❖ **1892**
  - ➤ Inspects Indian Reservations.

- ❖ **1894**
  - ➤ Elliot Roosevelt – his brother, passes away.
  - ➤ Son Archibald is born to Theodore and Edith.

- ❖ **1895**
  - ➤ Elected President of the Board of Police Commissioners.

- ❖ **1897**
  - ➤ Publishes *American Ideals*.
  - ➤ Becomes Assistant Secretary of the Navy by the President of the United States, William McKinley.
  - ➤ Another son born to Theodore and Edith – Quentin.

- ❖ **1898**
  - ➤ Joins the first United States Volunteer Cavalry Regiment.

- Serves in Spanish-American War; promoted to Colonel.
- Nominated and elected to the Governor of New York State by the Republican Party.

❖ 1900

- Nominated to Republican presidential ticket as vice president.
- Elected Vice President of the United States to William McKinley.

❖ 1901

- President McKinley is shot.
- Roosevelt becomes President of the United States.
- He is the 26th president and youngest to hold the position.

❖ 1902

- Starts first of 45 antitrust suits to dissolve business monopolies.

❖ 1903

- Establishes first federal bird reserve.
- Signs Treaty with Panama to build the Panama Canal.

- ❖ **1904-1905**
  - ➤ Re-elected to the office of the president.
  - ➤ Establishes United States Forest Service.
  - ➤ Establishes first federal game reserve.
  - ➤ Negotiates the Russo-Japanese Peace Treaty.

- ❖ **1906**
  - ➤ Establishes a list of national parks and monuments.
  - ➤ Given Nobel Peace Prize for mediation of the Russo-Japanese War.

- ❖ **1908**
  - ➤ Appoints National Conservations Commission.

- ❖ **1909**
  - ➤ Presidency comes to an end.
  - ➤ Interest and celebrity increases even though he leaves office.

- ❖ **1910**
  - ➤ Accepts Nobel Peace Prize in Norway.

- ❖ **1912**
  - ➢ Is petitioned to accept nomination for president from the Republican Party.
  - ➢ Nominated Presidential Candidate of Progressive Party; after Republican nomination goes to Howard Taft.
  - ➢ Shot in the chest yet does not perish from wound.
  - ➢ Loses Presidential Election to Woodrow Wilson.

- ❖ **1913**
  - ➢ Publishes *Theodore Roosevelt – An Autobiography and History as Literature and Other Essays*.

- ❖ **1914**
  - ➢ Nearly dies due to a leg injury sustained while hunting.

- ❖ **1916**
  - ➢ Declines progressive presidential nomination and puts support behind the Republican candidate.

- ❖ **1918**
  - ➢ Publishes *The Great Adventure*.

- ❖ **1919**
  - ➢ Passes in his sleep due to a coronary embolism; or a blood clot; he was 60 years old.

References

Baer, D., & Feloni, R. (2014). 15 Teddy Roosevelt quotes on courage, leadership, and success. Business Insider. https://www.businessinsider.in/15-teddy-roosevelt-quotes-on-courage-leadership-and-success/articleshow/50987984.cms

Morris, E. (2001). The Rise of Theodore Roosevelt. Random House Trade Paperbacks.

Roosevelt, T. (2006). An Autobiography by Theodore Roosevelt. http://www.freeinfosociety.com/media/pdf/4503.pdf

Theodore Roosevelt: The 26th President of the United States. (2021). The White House. https://www.whitehouse.gov/about-the-white-house/presidents/theodore-roosevelt/

Theodore Roosevelt. (2021). Theodore Roosevelt Center. https://www.theodorerooseveltcenter.org/